WITHDRAWN

CAREER EXPLORATION

Veterinarian

by Michael Burgan

Consultant:
Daniel F. Simpson, D.V.M.
West Bay Animal Hospital
Warwick, Rhode Island

CAPSTONE BOOKS
an imprint of Capstone Press
Mankato, Minnesota

Capstone Books are published by Capstone Press
151 Good Counsel Drive, P.O. Box 669, Mankato, Minnesota 56002
http://www.capstone-press.com

Library of Congress Cataloging-in-Publication Data
Burgan, Michael
    Veterinarian/by Michael Burgan.
    p. cm.—(Career Exploration)
    Includes bibliographical references (p. 45) and index.
    Summary: Introduces the career of veterinarian, discussing educational
requirements, duties, work environment, salary, employment outlook, and possible
future positions.
    ISBN 0-7368-0493-5
    1. Veterinarians—Juvenile literature. 2. Veterinary medicine—Vocational
guidance—Juvenile literature. [1. Veterinarians. 2. Veterinary medicine—Vocational
guidance. 3. Vocational guidance.] I. Title. II. Series.

SF756 .B87 2000
813'.54—dc21   99-053969

Editorial Credits

Connie R. Colwell, editor; Steve Christensen, cover designer; Kia Bielke,
    production designer and illustrator; Heidi Schoof, photo researcher

Photo Credits

FPG International LLC/C. Jeffry Myers, 30
James P. Rowan, 18
Photo Network/Phyllis Picardi, 40
Photri Microstock, cover, 28
Root Resources/Pat Wadecki, 20
Tom Stack & Associates/Tom and Therisa Stack, 22
Unicorn Stock Photos, 32
University of Minnesota/Michelle Mero Riedel, 6, 8, 11, 12, 14, 17, 25, 35, 38, 43

1 2 3 4 5 6 05 04 03 02 01 00

Table of Contents

Fast Facts

Career Title	Veterinarian
O*NET Number	32114B
DOT Cluster (Dictionary of Occupational Titles)	Professional, technical, and managerial occupations
DOT Number	073.101-010
GOE Number (Guide for Occupational Exploration)	02.03.03
NOC Number (National Occupational Classification-Canada)	3114
Salary Range (U.S. Bureau of Labor Statistics and Human Resources Development Canada, late 1990s figures)	U.S.: $29,900 to $100,000 Canada: $22,600 to $60,000 (Canadian dollars)
Minimum Educational Requirements	U.S.: veterinary school degree plus specialty training Canada: veterinary school degree plus specialty training
Certification/Licensing Requirements	U.S.: mandatory Canada: mandatory

4

Subject Knowledge	Mathematics; chemistry; biology; psychology; medicine and dentistry; therapy and counseling; education and training; English; philosophy and theology; public safety and security
Personal Abilities/Skills	Logic and scientific thinking; ability to stay calm; ability to use eyes, hands, and fingers with skill and accuracy; ability to make important decisions based on fact and own judgment
Job Outlook	U.S.: faster than average growth Canada: good
Personal Interests	Scientific: interest in discovering, collecting, and analyzing information about the natural world and in applying scientific research findings to problems in medicine, life sciences, and natural sciences
Similar Types of Jobs	Animal trainers; animal breeders; veterinary technicians; chiropractors; dentists, optometrists; physicians; research scientists

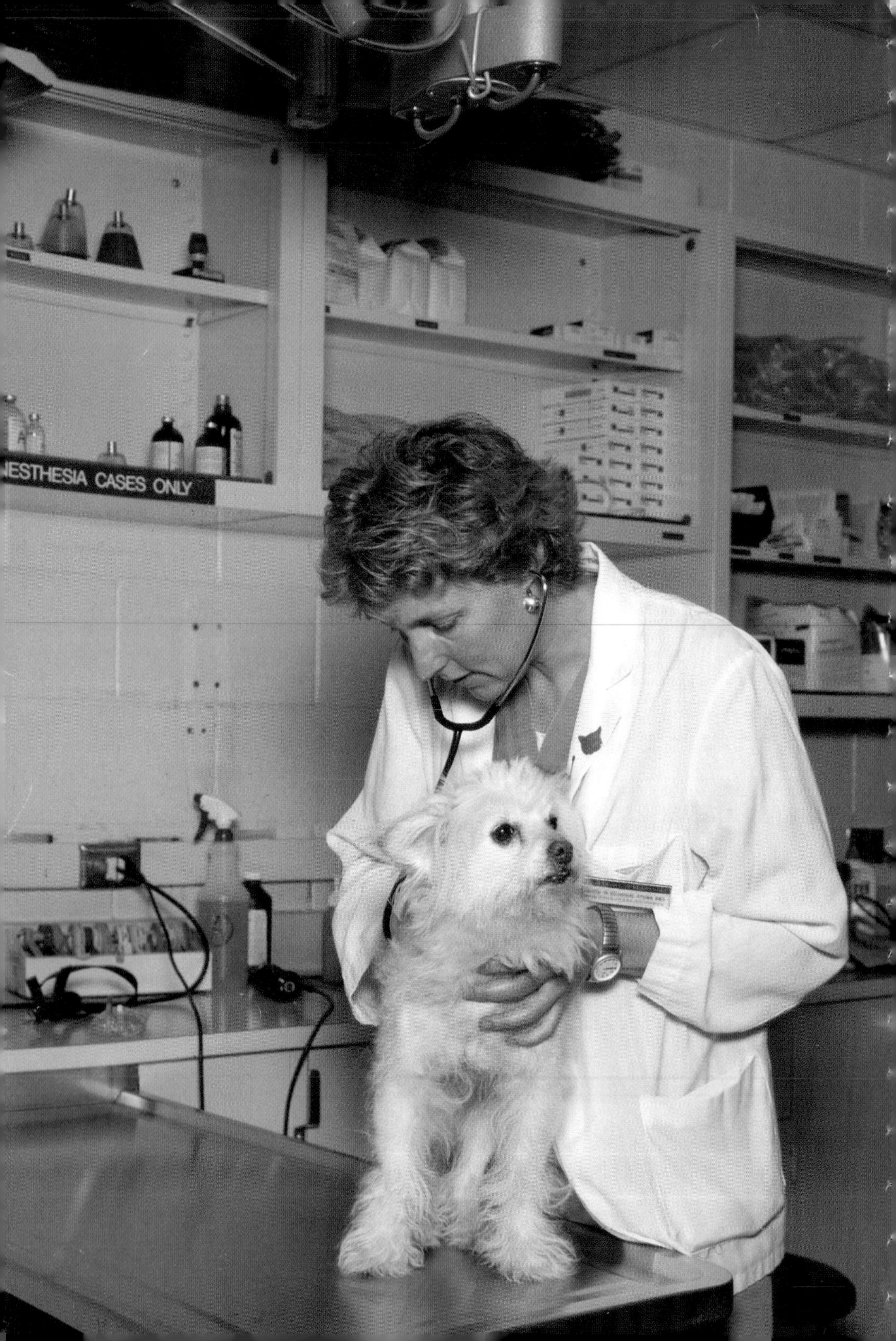
NESTHESIA CASES ONLY

Chapter 1

Veterinarians

Veterinarians are doctors who care for animals. Veterinarians sometimes are called doctors of veterinary medicine (D.V.M.).

Veterinarians may care for pets, farm animals, or animals that live in zoos or aquariums. Some veterinarians even care for wild animals.

Job Responsibilities

Veterinarians perform many of the same tasks as medical doctors. Veterinarians perform checkups, treat diseases, repair injuries, and perform operations. But veterinarians perform these tasks on animals instead of people.

Veterinarians often give animals vaccines. These medicines help prevent various diseases. Veterinarians usually inject vaccines into animals

Veterinarians often care for pets.

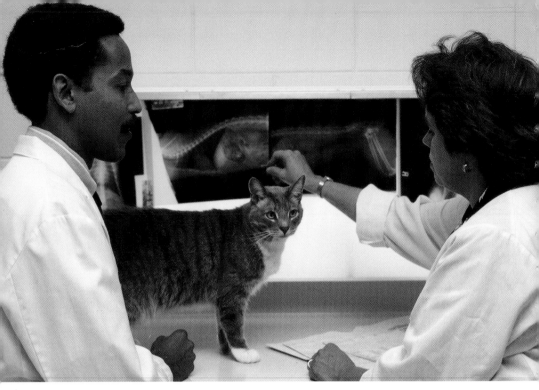

X-rays can show veterinarians exactly where an animal's bone has broken.

with a needle. Veterinarians give some vaccines every year. They give other vaccines less often.

Veterinarians use x-ray machines to examine animals that might have broken bones. These machines take pictures of animals' bones and organs. X-rays can show veterinarians exactly where an animal's bone has broken. Veterinarians then can set bones so they will heal properly.

Veterinarians use ultrasound machines to look for other problems inside an animal's body. Ultrasound machines use sound waves to produce images of soft tissues such as the heart and liver.

Veterinarians sometimes must operate on animals. They may need to repair wounded organs or muscles. They may need to remove diseased cells. They also may operate on animals to prevent them from breeding.

Veterinarians must give animals an anesthetic before operations. This drug puts animals to sleep and prevents them from feeling pain during operations. Veterinarians usually inject the anesthetic into animals with a needle. Veterinarians also can give the anesthetic to animals through a breathing tube or mask.

Other Duties

Veterinarians must get along well with animal owners. Animal owners often need advice or have questions about their animals. Veterinarians may suggest special diets for animals. They may offer tips to stop animals' bad behaviors. Veterinarians also help people who are upset about their sick or injured pets.

Tools

Veterinarians use many of the same tools as other medical doctors. Veterinarians use a thermometer to take an animal's temperature. They use an otoscope to check an animal's ears. They use a stethoscope to listen to an animal's heart and lungs. Veterinarians also use an ophthalmoscope to check an animal's eyes. These tools help give veterinarians an idea of an animal's general health.

Veterinarians use other tools for operations. They use special knives called scalpels to cut through animals' skin or organs. Veterinarians also use clamps of different sizes. Clamps can stop the flow of blood or hold back skin. Veterinarians use special threads called sutures to sew up cuts.

Specialties

Some veterinarians specialize in one kind of animal medicine. These veterinarians must have the skills and knowledge needed for their specialty. For example, a veterinarian may

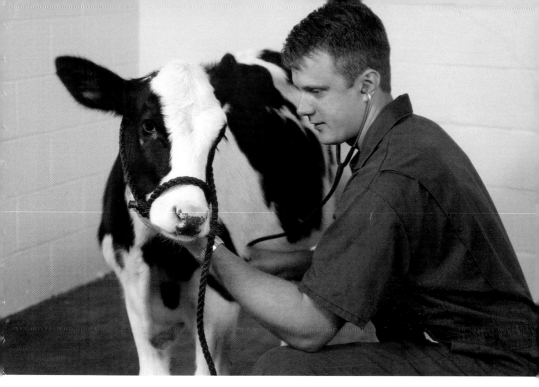

Veterinarians use a stethoscope to listen to an animal's heart and lungs.

specialize in dental care. Dental veterinarians know about different animals' teeth and mouths. These veterinarians use special tools to clean or remove teeth. Other veterinarians specialize in cardiology. These veterinarians must know how to treat animals' hearts.

Other veterinarians specialize in treating one kind of animal. Equine veterinarians care for horses. Feline veterinarians care for cats. Such specialists must be experts in the

Some veterinarians care for animals at zoos.

different health problems that affect particular animals.

Employment Areas

Most veterinarians in North America work in private practice. These veterinarians have their own offices or clinics or work with other veterinarians. They usually care for companion animals. These animals usually are called pets.

Dogs, cats, and birds are the most common companion animals.

Other veterinarians in private practice care for farm animals such as cows and pigs. These veterinarians often visit animals on farms. A small number of veterinarians treat both farm and companion animals.

Some veterinarians work at zoos, animal parks, or aquariums. Most large zoos have their own full-time veterinarians. Veterinarians who work for zoos and animal parks may care for a wide range of animals.

Other veterinarians work for the government or private companies. These veterinarians may check the health of animals raised for food or products such as eggs and milk. They may do research on drugs used to treat animals and humans. Government veterinarians may study diseases that affect animals. They also may care for animals used in research projects.

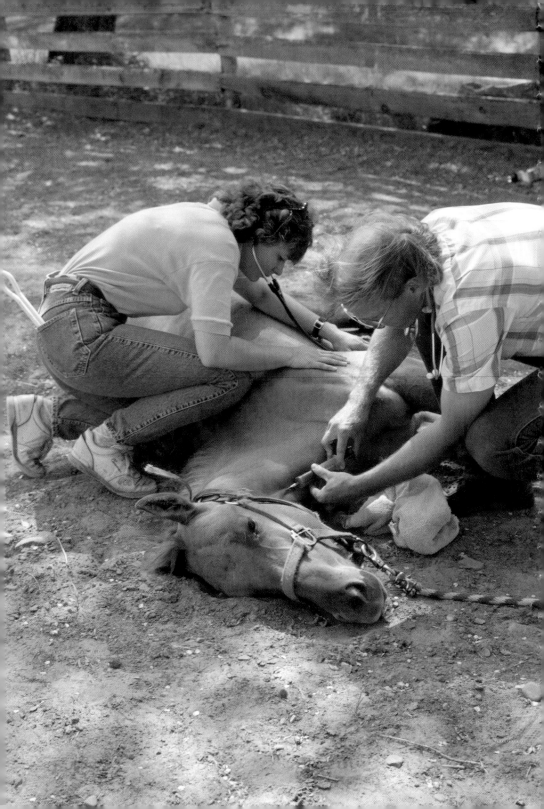

Chapter 2

Day-to-Day Activities

Veterinarians can work in many places. Veterinarians use many of the same skills no matter where they work. But veterinarians' daily tasks may vary depending on their work settings.

Veterinarians in Private Practice

Most veterinarians work in private practice. Many veterinarians in private practice work with companion animals. Other veterinarians in private practice treat farm animals.

Companion animal veterinarians spend most of their time performing outpatient care. For this care, owners bring animals into the office for checkups or tests. Some animals may

Veterinarians' daily tasks depend on their work settings.

appear sick. Veterinarians try to diagnose these animals' illnesses. They may ask the owner about the animal's general behavior. They also may ask about the animal's eating, bladder, and bowel habits. Veterinarians examine the animal carefully. They may use a needle to remove a small amount of the animal's blood. Veterinarians perform tests on this blood. These tests often help the veterinarians determine what is wrong with the animal. Veterinarians then may prescribe medicine or other treatment for the animal.

Veterinarians may need to give injured or sick animals inpatient treatment. These animals must stay at a veterinary clinic or hospital for a period of time. Inpatient care may involve surgery. Surgery often involves health risks to animals. For example, the anesthetic can cause side effects such as vomiting. Animals that receive anesthetic often must remain at veterinary clinics or hospitals to recover from the effects of surgery. This helps make sure that the animals are physically ready to return home.

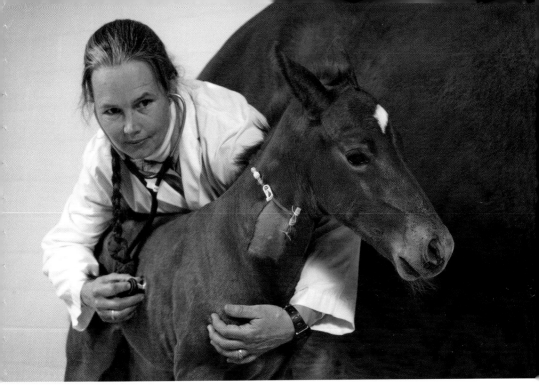

Veterinarians who care for farm animals often live in rural areas.

Veterinarians who care for farm animals often live in rural areas. Farm animals such as sheep, pigs, and cows also are called livestock. People raise these animals for food or products such as eggs and milk. Veterinarians who care for livestock often drive to farms to examine animals. Livestock veterinarians may give vaccines or treat illnesses. They may help a farm animal give birth to young. They even may perform surgery on farm animals.

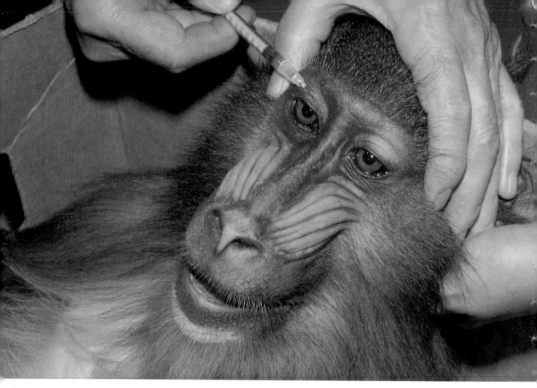

Veterinarians in zoos must know how to care for a variety of animals.

Veterinarians in Zoos

Veterinarians in zoos must know how to care for a variety of animals. They may have to treat a hippopotamus from Africa or a polar bear from the Arctic. These veterinarians perform many of the same tasks as other veterinarians.

Zoo veterinarians may have special challenges. They may need to give an anesthetic to large, wild animals. It can be dangerous to approach these animals.

Veterinarians usually use a dart gun to shoot the anesthetic into the animals. Veterinarians then can treat the animals once the anesthetic has put the animals to sleep.

Zoo veterinarians have other special concerns. Some zoo animals once lived in their natural environments. These animals were not near humans or the diseases they carry. Zoo animals also may not have been exposed to diseases carried by other animals. Zoo animals may not recover from these diseases. Zoo veterinarians try to prevent animals from getting these diseases.

Zoo veterinarians also may be concerned with how zoo animals breed and reproduce. It is difficult for some animals to produce young when they are not living in their natural environments. Zoo veterinarians try to create the right conditions to help these animals reproduce.

Veterinarians in Government Work

Many government agencies hire veterinarians. These veterinarians may work for federal, provincial, state, or local agencies. They also may work for the military. Some military units

Some veterinarians study animals in their natural environments.

keep animals such as dogs and horses. Military veterinarians care for these animals.

Many veterinarians who work for a federal, state, or provincial government agency perform research in laboratories. They may try to find ways to prevent and cure animal diseases. They also may help develop improved breeds of animals. For example, these veterinarians may develop a sheep that produces more wool or a cow that produces more milk. They also may examine animals raised for food or products.

Veterinarians make sure these animals are healthy. Part of this job includes examining animals from foreign countries. Veterinarians must make sure these animals are not bringing new diseases into North America.

Veterinarians in Research and Teaching

Some veterinarians perform research at universities or companies. These veterinarians often try to understand why animals become sick. They may look for ways to treat illnesses. They may develop medicines and healthy foods that fight animal diseases. These veterinarians also care for animals used for medical tests.

Some veterinarians study animals in their natural environments. Some of these research veterinarians work with endangered species. These animals are in danger of becoming extinct. Animals that are extinct no longer live anywhere in the world. Veterinarians study endangered animals' health to help them survive.

Research veterinarians also may teach at veterinary schools at colleges and universities. These veterinarians also usually perform research at the universities or colleges.

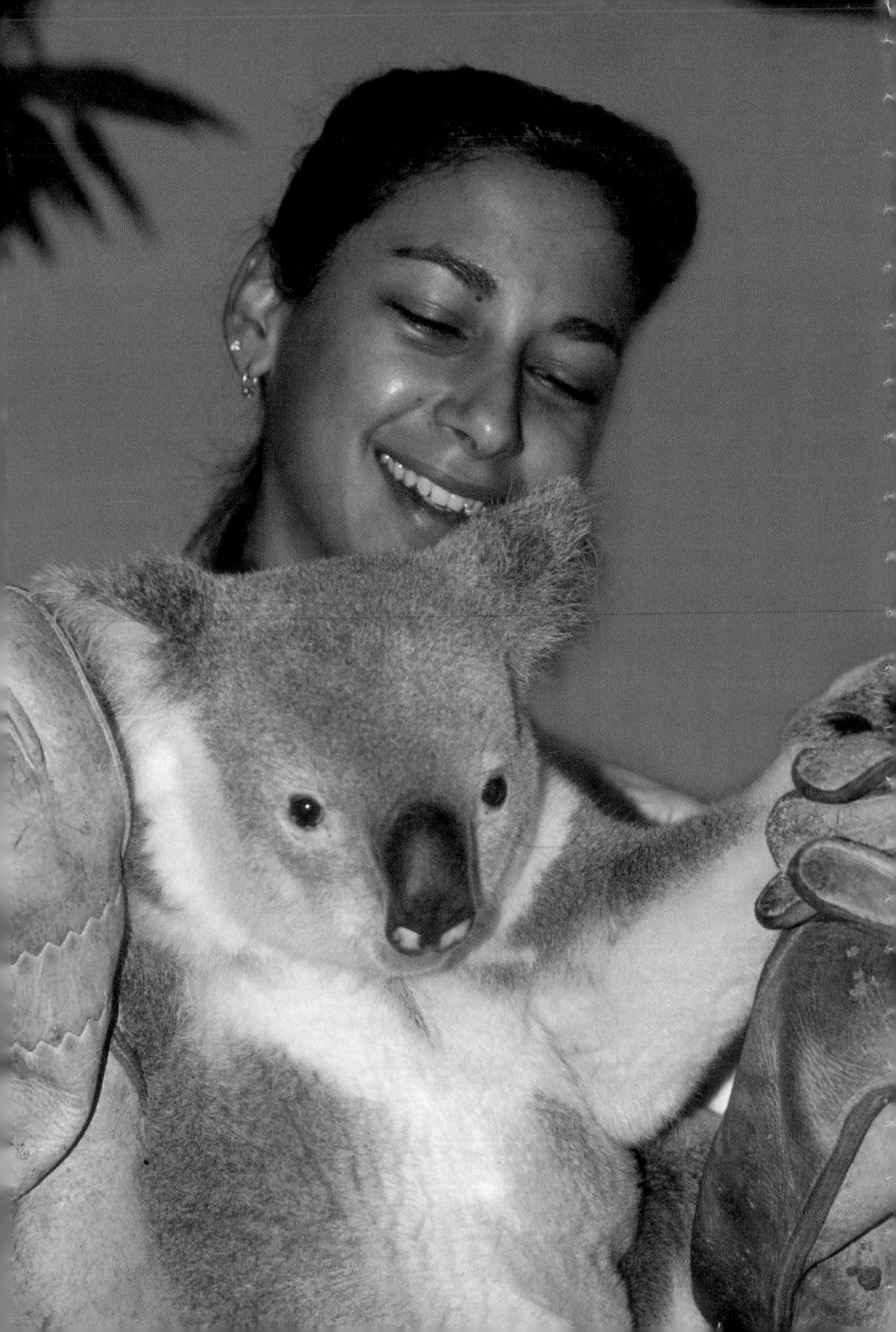

Chapter 3

The Right Candidate

Veterinarians' interests and skills may vary depending on their jobs. But most veterinarians share some basic interests and skills.

Major Interests and Skills
Veterinarians must like to work with animals. Most veterinarians work directly with animals. They must be able to comfort sick animals and handle upset animals.

Veterinarians must have an interest in science. Their work combines chemistry, biology, and other areas of science. Chemistry is the study of the substances that make up the earth. Biology is the study of all living things.

Veterinarians need other thinking skills. They often use logic in their work. This careful and

Veterinarians must like to work with animals.

23

correct reasoning helps veterinarians solve problems. Veterinarians also must carefully analyze data such as test results. These skills are necessary to treat and diagnose illnesses. They also are useful for researchers searching for cures for diseases.

Veterinarians must be willing to work many hours. Veterinarians sometimes must respond to emergencies at night. They might have to spend many hours taking care of sick animals or performing surgeries. This work can be difficult.

Veterinarians must be willing to accept physical dangers. Animals might scratch, kick, or bite when they are sick or afraid. Veterinarians can use drugs to calm down some animals. Veterinarians also risk becoming infected by sick animals. They wear face masks and rubber gloves to reduce the risk of catching diseases.

People Skills

Veterinarians must work well with people. Animal owners need to trust their animals' doctors. Veterinarians must earn owners' trust.

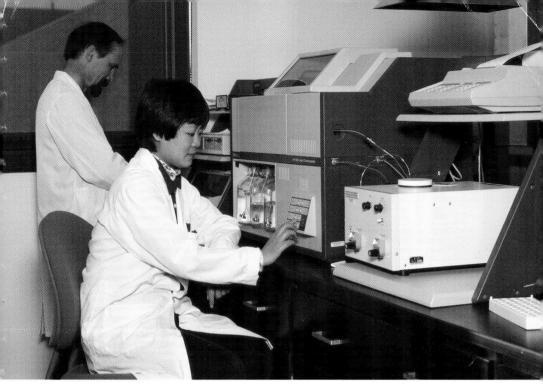

Veterinarians must be able to analyze data such as test results carefully.

They must be both skilled and honest to earn this trust.

Veterinarians must be compassionate. They may need to comfort owners who become upset about animals' accidents or illnesses. Veterinarians sometimes must inform owners if animals die. They should show concern for animal owners.

Veterinarians also must work well with other people in their field. Veterinarians must work well with the aides and technicians who work for them.

Skills

Workplace Skills   Yes / No

Resources:
Assign use of time .... ☑ ☐
Assign use of money .... ☑ ☐
Assign use of material and facility resources .... ☑ ☐
Assign use of human resources .... ☑ ☐

Interpersonal Skills:
Take part as a member of a team .... ☑ ☐
Teach others .... ☑ ☐
Serve clients/customers .... ☑ ☐
Show leadership .... ☑ ☐
Work with others to arrive at a decision .... ☑ ☐
Work with a variety of people .... ☑ ☐

Information:
Acquire and judge information .... ☑ ☐
Understand and follow legal requirements .... ☑ ☐
Organize and maintain information .... ☑ ☐
Understand and communicate information .... ☑ ☐
Use computers to process information .... ☑ ☐

Systems:
Identify, understand, and work with systems .... ☑ ☐
Understand environmental, social, political, economic,
    or business systems .... ☑ ☐
Oversee and correct system performance .... ☑ ☐
Improve and create systems .... ☑ ☐

Technology:
Select technology .... ☑ ☐
Apply technology to task .... ☑ ☐
Maintain and troubleshoot technology .... ☐ ☑

Foundation Skills

Basic Skills:
Read .... ☑ ☐
Write .... ☑ ☐
Do arithmetic and math .... ☑ ☐
Speak and listen .... ☑ ☐

Thinking Skills:
Learn .... ☑ ☐
Reason .... ☑ ☐
Think creatively .... ☑ ☐
Make decisions .... ☑ ☐
Solve problems .... ☑ ☐

Personal Qualities:
Take individual responsibility .... ☑ ☐
Have self-esteem and self-management .... ☑ ☐
Be sociable .... ☑ ☐
Be fair, honest, and sincere .... ☑ ☐

They may need to talk to specialists to get information about wild animals or unusual illnesses. Research veterinarians often work as part of a team. These researchers must work closely with others in order to complete projects.

Other Skills

Veterinarians must have good judgment. They must respond quickly to difficult situations. Veterinarians must decide the best treatments for diseases. Their decisions might mean life or death for a sick animal.

Veterinarians must have good communication skills. They need to speak and write clearly. Aides, technicians, animal owners, and other veterinarians need to understand veterinarians' instructions. These instructions must be both clear and exact.

Veterinarians must work well with their hands. They need to be steady and accurate when using surgical tools such as scalpels and clamps. They also need to handle animals carefully during examinations and treatments.

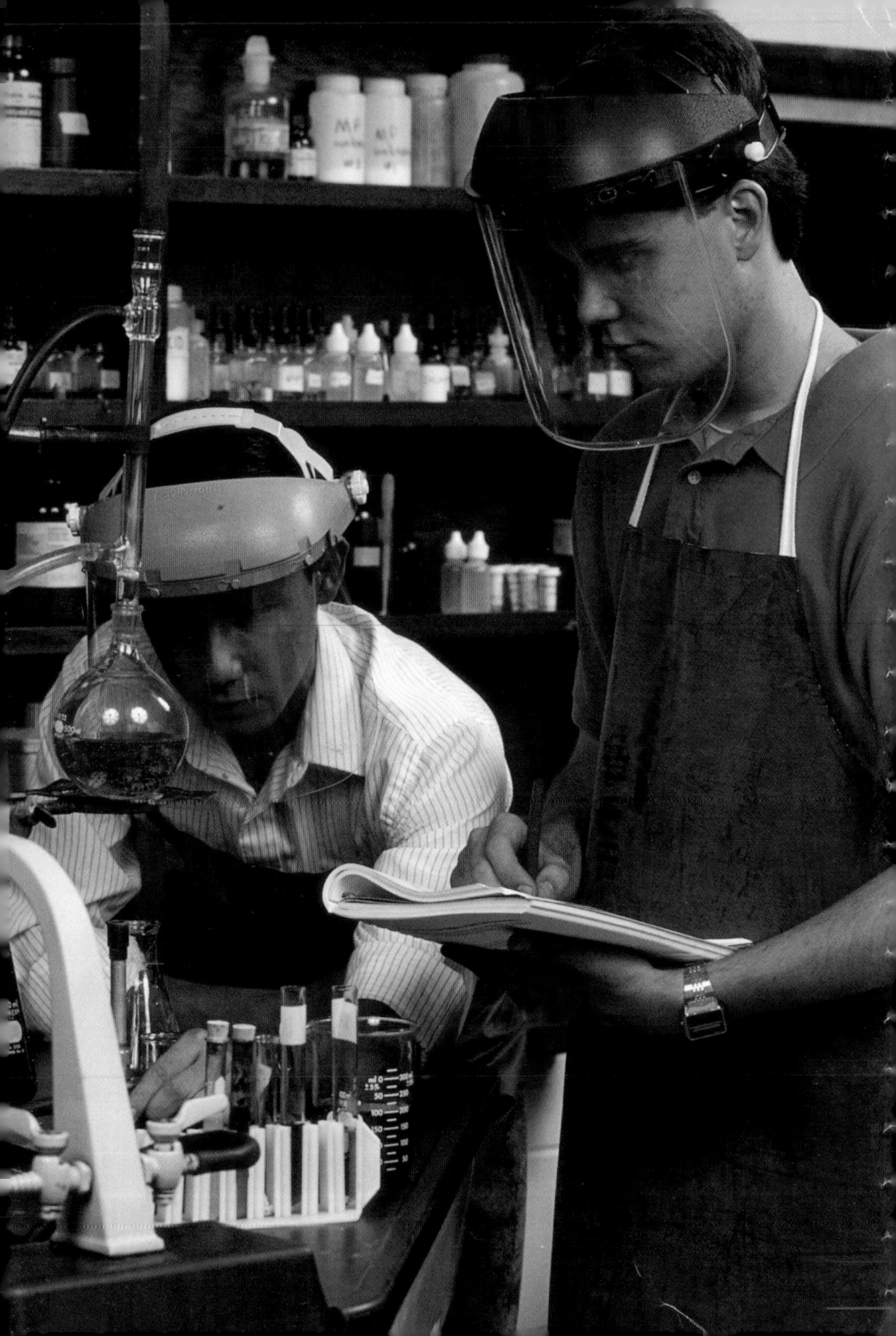

Chapter 4

Preparing for the Career

People who want to be veterinarians must be prepared for their careers. They must attend a college or university before attending veterinary school. They then must earn a license to practice veterinary medicine in their state or province.

High School Education

High school students who want to become veterinarians should take a variety of classes. Classes in math and science are most important. Science classes should include chemistry, biology, and physics. Physics is the study of matter and energy. These classes prepare students for college.

Students must attend a college or university before going to veterinary school.

High school students should take science classes to prepare for a career as a veterinarian.

Other classes also are important for future veterinarians. English and communication classes teach students to speak and write well. Business and computer courses will help veterinarians who hope to run their own practices.

It is beneficial for high school students to work with animals. Some schools offer classes in vocational agriculture. These classes teach students about farming and livestock. Students also can join clubs such as 4-H or Future Farmers of America. These clubs give students experience with farming and livestock.

Some part-time jobs allow students to work with animals. Students may work at livestock farms or kennels. Kennels are businesses that raise and train companion animals. They also care for animals whose owners are away. Some veterinarians hire students to perform office tasks. Students can learn many things about animals and veterinary medicine at such jobs.

Pre-Veterinarian Education

After high school, students must prepare for veterinary school by attending a college or university. In the United States, all future veterinarians earn a bachelor's degree from a college or university. Students usually complete these degrees in four years of study. In Canada, many veterinary students take two years of college or university study.

Students who hope to enter veterinary school sometimes are called pre-vet students.

Students who want to enter veterinary school sometimes are called pre-vet students.

Pre-vet students take many science courses in areas such as biology and chemistry. Students also may take courses not related to science such as English or history.

Many pre-vet students attend a college of agriculture. These colleges usually are at large state universities. Agricultural colleges teach about farming and livestock. They offer many courses that are helpful for future veterinarians.

Pre-vet students benefit from working with animals. They can learn about research by working in college research laboratories. Pre-vet students may care for animals that live in these laboratories. Students also may assist with experiments.

Pre-vet students must earn good grades. It is difficult for students to gain admission into veterinary schools. The United States has only 27 veterinary schools. Canada has only four veterinary schools. The schools cannot accept all the students who apply. Pre-vet students usually have a B average or better in their college courses. Pre-vets also must score well on veterinary school admission tests. These tests include the Graduate Record Examination and the Veterinary College Admission Test.

Veterinary School

Veterinarians must earn a Doctor of Veterinary Medicine (D.V.M.) degree at a veterinary school before they can begin work. All veterinary schools teach similar topics. Students learn how diseases spread and how these diseases affect animals. They learn how to use the tools needed to practice veterinary medicine. Students also study different kinds of animals. They learn how the animals' bodies work.

Veterinary students spend time in different school settings. Students spend much of their first two years in classrooms. They then spend more time in laboratories or working directly with animals.

Some veterinarians choose a specialty. For example, a veterinarian may specialize in feline veterinary medicine. Another veterinarian may specialize in surgery. Veterinarians with specialties must work as interns for a year to learn these additional skills. Interns often are not paid for their work.

Some veterinarians become board certified. To be board certified, veterinarians must study their specialty an additional two or three years. Board-certified veterinarians include surgeons, cardiologists, and exotic small animal veterinarians. Exotic animals are animals that few people keep as pets.

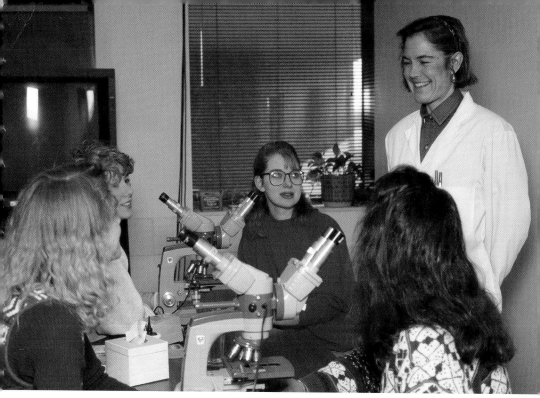

Veterinary students spend much of their first two
years in classrooms.

Licensing

Almost all veterinarians in the United
States and Canada must be licensed. Some
veterinarians in government work do not have
to be licensed.

To become licensed in the United States,
veterinarians first must pass the National
Board Examination (NBE). This test has 400

High
School
Diploma

Bachelor's
Degree

general questions about veterinary medicine. Veterinarians then must pass the Clinical Competency Test (CCT). This test has 14 questions about real-life veterinary situations. The CCT helps show how well veterinarians solve problems and make veterinary decisions.

Canada's NBE has both 400 written questions and 14 problems to be solved. The Canadian NBE also has a third part. It tests veterinarians at an actual clinic or hospital. Not all veterinarians are required to take this part. Veterinarians who pass the NBE can apply for licenses in their province.

In Quebec, veterinarians have different requirements than in other provinces. The

D.V.M. Degree → Licensing

Ordre des médecins vétérinaires du Québec oversees the licensing and certification of veterinarians in Quebec.

Continuing Education

Veterinarians must be willing to continue to learn about veterinary medicine throughout their careers. Some states and provinces require veterinarians to take extra courses to keep their licenses.

Veterinarians also may read books and magazines or attend conferences that deal with their profession. This helps veterinarians keep up with changes in science that affect veterinary medicine.

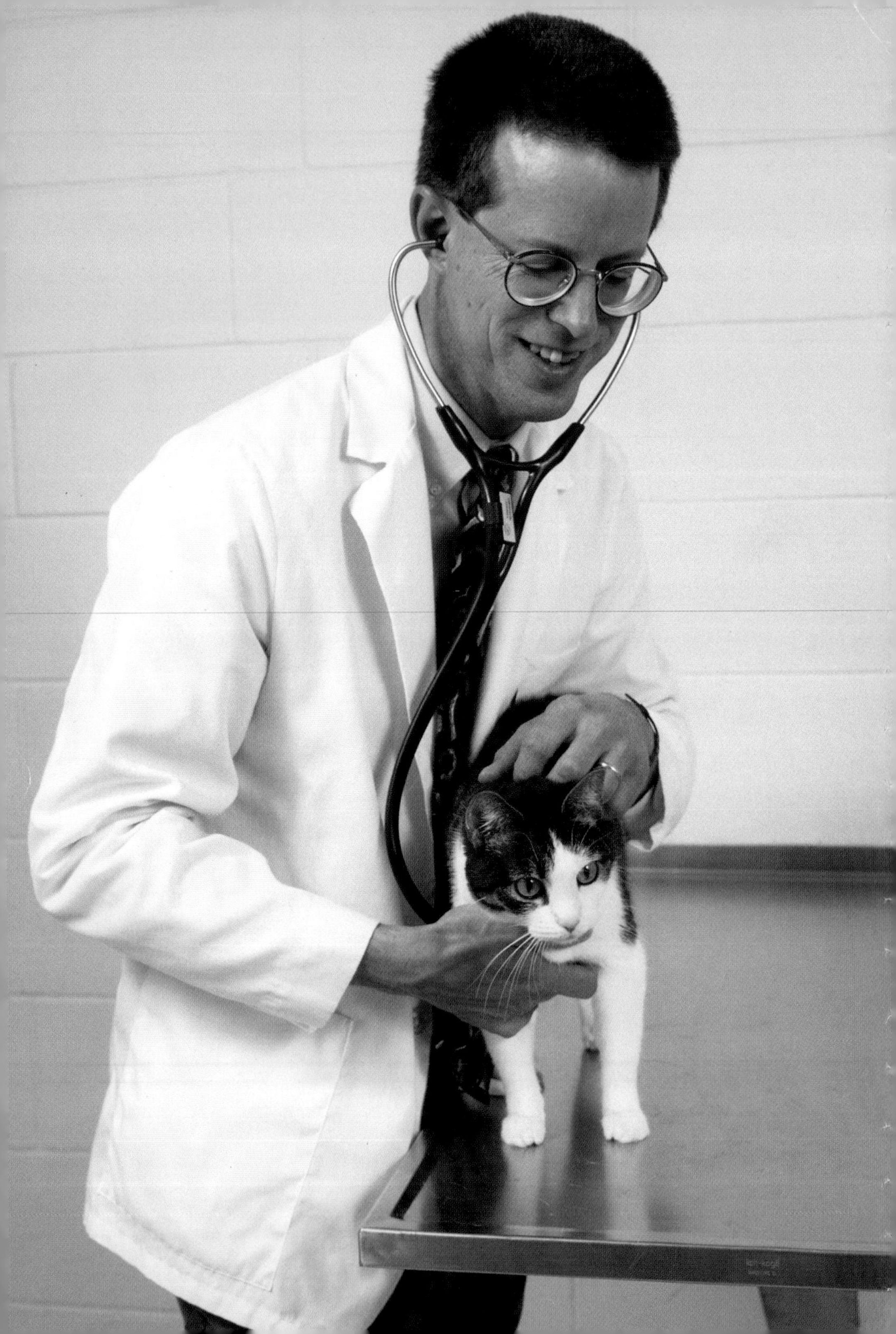

Chapter 5

The Market

The job market for veterinarians depends on where they work and their specialties. Veterinarians' salaries and advancement opportunities also depend on their locations and specialties.

Salary

In the United States, veterinarians have a wide range of salaries. Much of this range depends on veterinarians' specialties. U.S. veterinarians earn between $29,900 and $100,000 per year. The average salary for veterinarians in private practice is about $50,075 per year.

In Canada, the salary range for veterinarians is between $22,600 and $60,000. The average salary for veterinarians in Canada is $41,100 per year.

The job market for veterinarians depends on where they work.

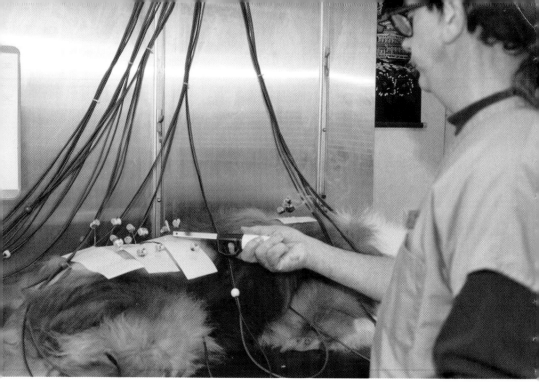
Veterinary acupuncturists use needles to relieve pain or treat illnesses.

Job Outlook

In the United States, the number of jobs for veterinarians should grow faster than average. In Canada, the job outlook for veterinarians is good. New veterinarians will be needed to take the place of doctors who retire. New positions for veterinarians also will be created.

Many veterinarians care for companion animals. The number of companion animals increased greatly in recent years. In the future, the number of companion animals will probably increase at a slower rate. But companion animal veterinarians still must compete to find jobs. They may have to take jobs that require them to work nights and weekends.

Jobs for livestock veterinarians are expected to grow slowly. But these vets still may have an easier time finding jobs than companion animal veterinarians. Fewer veterinarians choose a farm animal specialty. There is less competition for such jobs.

Veterinarians who specialize likely will have more job opportunities. Today, more animal owners are willing to spend money for procedures such as surgery or cancer treatment. Cancer is a disease in which abnormal cells grow out of control. Owners also are trying non-traditional treatments for their animals. These include chiropractic care and acupuncture. Chiropractors make adjustments to animals' spines. Acupuncturists use needles to relieve pain or treat illnesses.

Few research job openings exist for veterinarians in government or with companies. But some growth in this field should occur. People still need veterinarians to work in food safety and disease prevention.

Advancement Opportunities

Veterinarians can advance by gaining experience and knowledge. Successful veterinarians may hire other veterinarians to work for them. They also may open additional clinics or offices.

Government veterinarians usually are paid according to their skills and experience. As they gain experience, these veterinarians may earn more money. Experienced veterinarians eventually may supervise other veterinarians. Veterinarians who work for companies also may have the chance to become managers. Managers usually earn higher salaries.

Veterinarians who teach also may advance. They can advance from assistant professors to associate or full professors. These professors may earn more pay and have more responsibilities. More experienced professors might take on administrative jobs. These professors may be in charge of a school department.

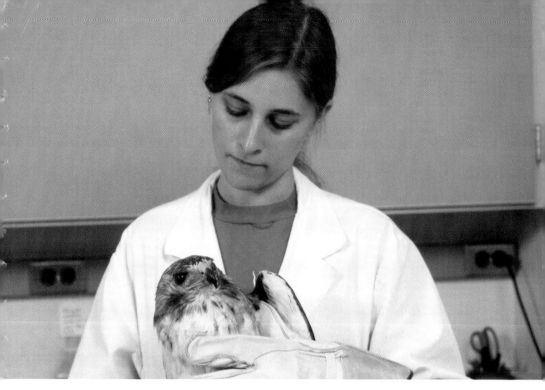

People who are interested in animals may work at zoos.

Related Careers

People who are interested in animals may work in a variety of careers. They may become animal breeders or trainers. They may work at zoos or aquariums. They also may become veterinary technicians. These people assist veterinarians with their jobs.

Animals help people in many ways. Some animals provide food and food products for people. Animals also provide companionship for people. In the future, veterinarians will continue to use their skills to help animals live better lives.

Words to Know

anesthetic (an-iss-THET-ik)—a drug that makes animals sleep so doctors can perform surgery on them

livestock (LIVE-stok)—animals raised on a farm for food, such as cows or pigs

ophthalmoscope (of-THUHL-muh-skope)—a tool veterinarians use to look into animals' eyes

scalpel (SKAL-puhl)—a small, sharp knife used by veterinarians to cut animals' skin

stethoscope (STETH-uh-skope)—a medical instrument used by veterinarians to listen to the sounds of animals' heart and lungs

vaccine (vak-SEEN)—a medicine given to animals to prevent them from catching a certain disease

To Learn More

Cosgrove, Holli, ed. *Career Discovery Encyclopedia.* Vol. 8. Chicago: Ferguson Publishing Company, 2000.

Lee, Mary Price and Richard S. Lee. *Opportunities in Animal and Pet Care Careers.* VGM Opportunities. Lincolnwood, Ill.: VGM Career Horizons, 1994.

Maze, Stephanie and Catherine O'Neill Grace. *I Want to Be a Veterinarian.* San Diego: Harcourt Brace, 1997.

Swope, Robert E. *Opportunities in Veterinary Medicine Careers.* VGM Opportunities. Lincolnwood, Ill.: VGM Career Horizons, 1993.

Useful Addresses

American Veterinary Medical Association
1931 North Meacham Road
Suite 100
Schaumburg, IL 60173

Canadian Veterinary Medical Association
339 Booth Street
Ottawa, ON K1R 7K1
Canada

Future Farmers of America
6060 FFA Drive
P.O. Box 68960
Indianapolis, IN 46268-0960

National Zoological Park
Department of Education and Volunteer Services
3001 Connecticut Avenue NW
Washington, DC 20008

Internet Sites

American College of Veterinary Surgeons
http://www.acvs.org

American Veterinary Medical Association
http://www.avma.org

Canadian Veterinary Medical Association
http://www.cvma-acmv.org

Job Futures—Physicians, Dentists, and
Veterinarians
http://www.hrdc-drhc.gc.ca/JobFutures/english/
volume1/311/311.htm

Occupational Outlook Handbook—
Veterinarians
http://stats.bls.gov/oco/ocos076.htm

Index